KEITH TYSON

Delfina, London

Published by Delfina, London
50 Bermondsey Street
London SE1 3UD
t +44 (0171) 357 6600
f +44 (0171) 357 0250
e-mail: admin@delfina.org.uk

British Library Cataloguing-in-Publication Data: a catalogue record
is available from the British Library.

Photographs of work by FXP, London.

Keith Tyson is represented by Anthony Reynolds Gallery, London

ISBN: 0 9535264 0 2

Delfina gratefully acknowledges financial support from
The Henry Moore Foundation

Design/Production: Alan Ward, Axis Design, Manchester.
e-mail: alan@axis.zen.co.uk

Printed by Craft Print Pte Ltd, Singapore, Singapore.

Knowing what to do next, that's always the problem. Of course, starting is a problem, but
Even before then, one must know to start, and how does one know that? How
Is that decision made? These are undoubtedly difficult questions (although I'm beginning
To doubt why I decided to start with them), but then their concern is fundamental
Human creativity, and there is little more difficult than that. It is beyond the scope of this
Text, and certainly beyond the scope of its author, to offer clear answers; and
Yet the questions clearly remain. Perhaps human creativity is simply the means by which answers, of
Sorts, are sought to the questions which its very existence raises, a perpetual examination of its
Own states, its own processes? But then what? What then? Yes, it's knowing what to do
Next, that's always the problem.

Every day there seems to be a new list. The earliest I saw was last year, flicking through a magazine in an airport shop (magazines like this are only bought in airports, it seems). It was American, *Life*. 'The 100 most important events & people of the past 1,000 years.' We begin with the events, at number 100 ('1582 — Fixing the Calendar'), past 82 ('1886 — Selling the World a Coke'), the invention of photography (37) and Gutenberg's bible (1). Despite this, Gutenberg himself does not make it into the list of the 100 most important people of the past 1,000 years, although the man deemed most important (need I say it's a man, an American man?) was an inventor also. And so it is not Darwin or Newton, Columbus or Luther (and one didn't really expect Ibn Battuta, Ibn Rushd or Ibn al-Haytham to figure prominently here). No,

the most important person of the past 1,000 years is Thomas Alva Edison, 1847–1931, inventor of recorded sound and the lightbulb.

What does this tell us? It tells us of the importance which society places upon technology, certainly, and the esteem in which we hold its inventors. (It also tells us a great deal about American pragmatism, but that is a different story.) That said, the decision to honour Edison in this way is laughable, or would be if it were not so despairing. The problem lies, to a great extent, with the structure of the survey, favouring, as it does, those cultures in which the achievements of the individual are valued above those of the community. Much Western technology — large sailing ships, double-entry book-keeping, optics, gunpowder, medicine, the

numeral zero — we owe to the Chinese, Indians and the Islamic world; we owe them much of our thinking too, with the translations by Muslim scholars of the texts of Greek Philosophy which had been neglected or suppressed by the Catholic Church for centuries. Even within *Life*, Gutenberg's primary achievement is described as devising the first Western movable-type system that worked; that the Koreans were using movable metal type the previous century, and the Chinese movable wooden type three hundred years before that, seems to matter little. What those in the East had failed to do was create a Western system.

Reputation is all, it seems. It is something that Edison knew well and so his presence here is useful. Edison was actually less a scientist or inventor than a businessman and publicist (he once said that he did-n't need to be much of a mathematician because he could always hire one). He learned to take advantage of the abilities of those around him, and no-one was more able than Nikola Tesla, a brilliant young Serbian whom Edison hired in 1883. Tesla worked hard, for long hours, improving Edison's primitive designs. When Tesla offered to redesign the company's elec-tric dynamos, Edison thought it a monumental task that would take years, and offered the Serb $50,000 if he managed it. Tesla completed it within twelve months; it was Edison who took the credit, however. As for the money: 'Tesla, you don't understand our American humour!' Edison hired the best people in their field, and he was mindful that their achieve-ments became his own. As he noted, 'Everybody steals in commerce and industry. I've stolen a lot myself. But I know *how* to steal.'

Let's steal ourselves away, and consider the artist as a type of inventor. Such a role was undoubtedly more widespread in the past, before the increased specialisation of knowledge began to split the arts and sciences (think of da Vinci, no.5 in the Top 100). In this century, Duchamp often thought of himself as an inventor; he first exhibited his roto-reliefs in an inventor's trade fair, with little success. There is John Cage, also, who took his position from Duchamp as much as his father (who was an inventor by profes-sion, albeit with little success either). And Keith Tyson? I'm not sure how Tyson considers his work compared to that of an inventor, but it might be use-ful for us to consider the relationship a little further.

Tyson's most important invention, if we may use the word here, is his Artmachine, a device which he often uses to help him make his work, or rather, to help him decide which work to make (it is a labour-making rather than a labour-saving device). When we think of 'machines', our vision is often fairly limited; for many, the word still conjures nineteenth-century visions of cogs and wheels, gears and levers. For some the vision has been upgraded, replaced with something modern, electric, electronic, compu-terised. Whatever, we still tend to think of machines as objects, objects that perform tasks, that do things for us. Perhaps we should think of these technologies in a slightly different way, paying more attention to 'software' rather than 'hardware'. Technology need not have a motor, nor a plug, yet this is still how most of us consider it. This is particularly true when (if) we consider some form of relationship between art and technology. In such circumstances, many still like to see a machine 'doing' something, performing, even if it is only a display upon a computer screen. Old preju-dices are transposed into a new situation, the new seen within the confines of the old (this is something McLuhan pointed out). As the visitor to an 'art and the computer' exhibition at the ICA put it in a 1968 New Scientist cartoon, 'I don't know much about *Cybernetic Serendipity* but I know what I like'.

Instead, Tyson has created his Artmachine from the most powerful technology known to humans: language. Some of this language does indeed exist on a computer, while some is contained in flow charts. As Tyson himself explains, 'it is probably most

helpful to imagine it as a complex set of rules that can access various sources of information such as libraries, the internet, et cetera, and use this informa-tion to create works in a wide range of styles and media.' As a machine it is infinetly expandable, and can produce an infinity of results, each differing slightly. Indeed, the mention of the library is reveal-ing. Tyson has often referred to Borges as an important influence upon the creation of the Artmachine (there are others) and perhaps it is his story 'The Library of Babel' which is most important here (although we shouldn't forget 'Tlön, Uqbar, Orbis Tertius', or 'The Garden of Forking Paths', or 'Pierre Menard, Author of the *Quixote*' or… or…).' 'The Universe (which others call the Library) is composed of an indefinite and perhaps infinite number of hexagonal galleries, with vast air shafts between, surrounded by very low railings.' Over many hundreds of years, the lifetimes of innumerable scholars, travellers, it becomes clear that all the books are made from the same elements — 'the space, the period, the comma, the 26 letters of the alphabet' — and that *there are no two identical books*. From this it is deduced that 'the Library is total and that its shelves register all the possible combinations of the twenty-odd orthographical symbols (a number which, though extremely vast, is not infinite): in other words, all that is given to express, in all languages.' This means that included is the true history of the future, the meaning of God, the story of one's death, even, hidden amongst a frightening number of volumes, the text which you are reading now: still more contain improved versions, a more accurate description here, a more elegant turn of phrase there; there are even versions, heaven forbid, less well written. Suffice it to say, the library contains everything, and its refutation.

Tyson's Artmachine is, to some extent, a part of Borges' Library (but then, we are all a part of Borges' Library). Rather, it shares with it a manner of operation, albeit in reverse, a narrowing of possibilities, the decision to take this, or that, forked path, until from an infinity of possible works, a single one is proposed (somewhere in Borges' Library there is a volume of the relationship between Tyson's work and Heisenberg's Uncertainty Principle although it has yet to be found). Tyson then becomes involved in the realisation of the work, in its materialisation; indeed, he seems to, if not delight, then to possess a certain pride in the level of physical attrition which such a procedure often requires of him. If Tyson can be seen as an inventor, it is not as the inventor of a simple object but of a complex process. While the machine has removed the difficulty of starting, of knowing what to do next, it has replaced this with the difficulty of stopping. As Jacques Ellul wrote in *The Technological Society*: 'The further the technical mechanism develops which allows us to escape natural necessity, the more we are subjected to artificial technical necessities.' We are all of us trapped within this labyrinth whether we recognise it or not, Tyson, myself, you, our critics, all of us.

* * *

Is this right? It is a large space, bright, wide, and contains many works, many different works. Along one wall is a large painting, very long, the thickness of the paint further extended by the thickness of the surface upon which it is applied. It is difficult to say if the painting is 'of' anything, although it could be a landscape; perhaps those are pieces of agricultural machinery. There is also a photograph, framed, of… silver foil? A figure? Against a silver foil background? It is difficult to see, difficult to tell. There's also a drawing, a panoramic vision upon drafting film, which shows some of the pieces which are in the gallery here. There are the desks from over there, and, yes, there's the photograph. The description reads: 'Artmachine Iteration: "The Development of Uniqueness in a Monomolecular Universe" (Number 1 — The Humming Bird) A photograph of a completely silver sculpture in a completely silver environment.' I thought it might help. It seems that all this work, each of these very different pieces, have been made by one person. Can this be right? There's a man over there on the video, talking enthusiastically. He seems to be trying to explain something.

I walk towards the two desks, two complete workstations with filing cabinet and pinboards, which have been placed next to each other. They appear identical, the papers, the pictures, even the scraps of masking tape on the filing cabinets. But then I begin to notice… yes, the graphs do show different readings, the photographs of a south London railway platform, though showing the same view, contain different people in different combinations

and, yes, the platform clock shows a different time. They are a minute apart, like the clocks on the desk here. The whole thing is a minute apart.

This is not the restrained dismissal of expressionism which Rauschenberg made with his replicated paint drips and while it shares, at least in part, a similar methodology with Douglas Heubler, it moves beyond it also. Rauschenberg's is replication, Heubler's reiteration, and Tyson's a reiteration further, a reiteration reiterated. As such, it seems to become less a sculptural installation than a performative one. I'm reminded of some of Cage's scores that require the use of radios during their performance. Of course, each performance of a scored piece of music is different, but that difference itself is seldom scored. Cage had a particular dislike of recorded music and his use of it within his works, whether on radio (for example, *Radio Music*, 1956) or records (such as the *Europera* series), was a means of re-energising the music, of loosening it, of allowing the possibility of chance within a preordained structure. It is within such a maxtrix that we find the birth of language.

I would like to add a footnote to that last remark, but footnote it here, with another's note. I have taken it from page 50 of Arthur Koestler's *The Act of Creation* (1970):

To page 40. The choice of the term 'matrix' is less easy to explain. In an earlier version I used 'field' and 'framework', but 'field' is too vague, and 'framework' too rigid. 'Matrix' is derived from the Latin for womb and is figuratively used for any pattern or mould in which things are shaped or developed, or type is cast. Thus the exercise of a habit or skill is 'moulded' by its matrix.

In mathematics, matrices are rectangular arrays of numbers capable of all sorts of magic; they can be subjected to various transformations without losing their identity — i.e. they are both 'flexible' and 'stable'.

He goes on but this much is fine, this is enough. The matrix is obviously important to Tyson. It's presence is clear in a work such as *Mount, seal and encapsulate, (A/1998/(u))* which consists of 'A found photograph sealed in progressive layers of wood, plaster, paper, paint and a final layer of associations originating from the memory of the photograph buried inside the box', that final layer a meshwork of words and connecting lines, each firing a reminiscence of others, like a memorial neural net. The matrix is confirmed in the vast electronic version of the piece, the word connections becoming Proustian dumb-bells connected by 1,200 feet of electrical cables. The matrix exists in the large square of floorboards, originally a site-specific piece in a London mews house, which becomes a large graph of time and space, the mark at its centre marking its own position within that continuum. The matrix is, of course, the Artmachine itself, a table of productive possibilities. And yet despite procreative derivation of the word, indeed the procreative actions of the thing itself, the matrix makes a secret of origins, it conceals the birth.

In Borges' story 'Tlön, Uqbar, Orbis Tertius' the narrator comes across one volume of the encyclopaedia of an unknown planet (it is an archetypically Borgesian story and tells us much about Tyson, as it does about many things). The culture of Tlön consists of one disciple, psychology, into which every other cultural movement has been subsumed. Literary critics often take two dissimilar books — 'the *Tao Te Ching* and *1001 Nights*, say' — and attribute them to the same author, thereby allowing them the possibility to ponder the psychology of such an individual. Faced with the diverse output of Keith Tyson, it is tempting to do the same. I fear its results would prove as useful as those of the Tlönians themselves. The beginning of the process is of little interest to Tyson (indeed, as I've hinted, the Artmachine is a means of getting past that initial stage). His interest lies further on, in the process, not in its end, but in its continuation. If Tyson is an inventor, then it is not as a problem-solver but as a problem-searcher. The Artmachine helps him find problems just as that other great matrix, the Library, helped its inhabitants similarly. Their expectations are shared. 'Obviously, no-one expects to discover anything.'

* * *

Ten Things (amongst many others) Randomly Presented for Keith Tyson:[1]

Keith Tyson is an artist concerned with the limits of unlimited things. He takes elements, whether formal or historical, constructive or conceptual and, through the determination of his Artmachine, a work of art is determined.

When I was thinking about the exhibition in Paris, I kept thinking about another exhibition, also in Paris. It was some time ago now, 1971, at Galerie Yvon Lambert. Then, the American artist Robert Barry had an exhibition which was announced by a mailer that read: 'Robert Barry presents three shows and a review by Lucy R. Lippard' (part of that review is reprinted here somewhere).

What happened in that space between the canvas and the stick being held in Jackson Pollock's hand? Why did those drips of paint fall in the way in which they did fall, in a process of auto-documentation? As in the famous illustration of chaos theory, were the ripples of paint affected by the childish screams of the boy Kosuth? (Chaos theory can often appear like determinism *in extremis*.) Tyson has said that his work operates within this small space, between chance and free-will, as deterministic interceptor.

'And I have some questions of my own. Is a review which is not published in a journal but constitutes part of an exhibition in itself a fake review? Can it view itself objectively? Or is it valid anyhow because people read it, because it does comment directly upon the show it is part of? Is the writer of such a review an artist even if she/he has made no art? If a writer calls what she/he does 'criticism', can anyone else call it art? Is the artist who 'presents' a writer's work as a minor part of this piece (the major part being the presentation per se) a critic himself? Is an artist ever not an artist if he/she says he or she is an artist? Does an artist have to make art?'

Like de Sade, Tyson does not break taboos in order simply to shock, but instead to allow a greater number of mathematical combinations.

1) Conceptual Artists are mystics rather than rationalists. They leap to conclusions that logic cannot reach.

5) Irrational thoughts should be followed absolutely and logically.

12) For each work of art that becomes physical there are many variations that do not.

35) These sentences comment on art, but are not art.

Sarah Gavlak: If, as you say, 'seduction is destiny', then is chance a result of seduction?

Jean Baudrillard: Of course. Chance is not at all a matter of luck, but the search for a privileged relation. The gambler turns himself into a strange attractor.

Each decision made using the art-machine, each path taken at each fork, is not simply the closing of another possibility but the closing of an infinity of possibilities. If it is decided that an element must be a, then it does not simply preclude a, but also $b, c, aa, az, 5, \int, ç, åå, ǎΩ, ∞…$ Any further decisions are made from this new position, decisions which move on a single stage while simultaneously abandoning the multitude which lay in wait, potentialities which shimmer transparently through the matrices of crystalline time.

The final form of Tyson's work cannot be determined in advance, but only when all the procedures of the Artmachine have been completed. While there remains an infinity of pieces which, this time, it has decided not to make, like the books in Borges' Library, there is also almost an infinity (almost an infinity?) of pieces which are almost identical to the finished piece, differentiated by only a shade of colour here, or the length of a line there. The same is true of this text, also, and it will become even more so after translation. In its original English, this piece is exactly one thousand words long. But how long will it be in French? How many differences will then emerge? These small transformations lie at the heart of Tyson's work, an exploration into differences both infinite and infinitessimal.

Since Goethe's Faust, our desire has been for Development. Of course, this has meant that our desires have also developed, but only insofar as they confirm our desire for Development. Like Capitalism, its obese off-spring good with numbers, Development possesses the ability to absorb indefinitely. There may be points of saturation, of micro-saturation, but the excess droplets are quickly, instantaneously, absorbed elsewhere.

Tyson's project is Faustian in many ways. My suggestion is not of some devilish pact (although that may explain his extraordinary work-rate). Instead, it is a measure of his immersion into a dynamic process that includes almost every mode of artistic expression, a process which assimilates all in its unending growth. Like Goethe's Faust, Tyson uses Development not simply to create money, fame or power (although they may be useful by-products) but as a resource for further Development, for experience, action, creativity. The capital thrown into circulation is himself.

To this end, he pursues the rationality of art capitalism to its ultimate conclusion, whereby its irrationality is all that is left (such are its contradictions). In a period when the production of 'variations on a theme', recognisable units of exchange, has become the dominant artistic mode, Tyson takes what is assumed a commercial necessity and forces it to become very nearly a liability. How do we recognise one of his works? Simply by the fact that no-one else would have made it? How do we know if we have a representative piece when all the pieces are perfectly representative, in their own way? Is it better to have an early or a late Tyson, and isn't the one implicated in the other anyway? Artists usually get better (or worse) the longer they've been working. Tyson will simply remain different, only more so. His achievement is to develop an art which has removed the illusion of progress.

Not art-in-progress but art-in-process.

*   *   *

Habit can be habit-forming, and that's not always a good thing. I think it was Beckett who wrote that habit is the ballast which chains a dog to its vomit, but then as Beckett often wrote about repetition, brilliantly, maybe that isn't such a bad thing after all. Artists have often introduced chance, random factors, into their work as a means of counteracting the seeming inevitability of habitual repetition. We could even repeat the same names by way of example: Duchamp's standard stoppages, firing paint-laden matchsticks from a toy cannon, pulling musical notes out of a hat for *Erratum Musical* (1913); Cage's use of the *I Ching* for the *Music of Changes* (1951–2) and many other compositions, both visual and musical, even the IC computer programme which simulated the *I Ching* and which Cage used from 1984. Some artists move into the opposite direction, making seriality an important element within their work (similarly, the list could go on and on). Of course, it is not really possible to separate the modes quite so cleanly. Tyson falls somewhere between the two, as do, it must be said, the other artists mentioned. Tyson's position, I believe, is a deliberate one. Tyson has got into the habit of using the Artmachine, of using chance, as a means of counteracting habit. He also makes works which have not been determined by the Artmachine as a means of counteracting the habit of using the Artmachine, although it remains to be seen whether this might also become habit-forming (you can see where this is going to get us). It is this relationship between structure and chance which is of real interest here. Cage's copy of the *I Ching* had a foreword by Jung:

We have not sufficiently taken into account as yet that we need the laboratory with its incisive restrictions in order to demonstrate the invariable validity of natural law. If we leave things to nature, we see a very different picture: every process is partially or totally interfered with by chance, so much so that under natural circumstances a course of events absolutely conforming to specific laws is almost an exception. [2]

This picture is only confirmed if we follow Jung into the laboratory. Alexander Fleming eventually discovered penicillin after two chance occurrences. The first was when, in 1922, his runny nose dripped into a dish and killed the bacilli in the culture; the second was when a spore of the mould *penicillium notatum* blew in through the open window and settled in a dish of staphylococci. As he was to say later, 'One sometimes finds what one is not looking for'. His scientific predecessor, Louis Pasteur, thought similarly: 'Chance only savours invention for minds which are prepared for discoveries by patient study and persevering efforts.'

Perhaps, in more everyday terms, we might say that these scientists 'made their own luck'. In many ways, this simply means having the intellectual means to recognise and then profit from occurences beyond our control. Being in 'the right place at the right time' is little more than recognising that this is the case and being in a position to take advantage. Luck most often comes to those who deserve it (but then, it must be said, there are those who are just lucky). Often, for Tyson, the relationship between perseverance and chance is the reverse of that described above. For the scientists, benevolent chance could be recognised only after a great deal of detailed and painstaking work. For Tyson, chance is often simply chosen at the beginning through the determination of the Artmachine; it is afterwards that the often awkward and painstaking work of its realisation takes place. It is important for Tyson — and it should be important to us also — that Tyson completes whatever is proposed by the Artmachine. If a work demands a certain process then that process must be carried out. Not to do so would be to fail the work; Tyson would instead be completing a different proposal, one of the almost infinitely 'similar' ones which the Artmachine could propose. I repeat, this is important for Tyson and it should be important to us also. It matters, it matters a great deal.

That last line has got me thinking, particularly as I was writing it while thinking of something else, of gambling. 'A great deal.' Gambling fascinates Tyson. In fact, I don't think he'd mind my saying that he is a gambler. Not just in the way he works, although it is evident there also (the risks he takes in showing some of those things!). No, I mean gambling proper, in the placing of bets. The use of systems in gambling is well-known (these systems, and their breakdown, is one of the things explored in James Flint's recent novel, *Habitus*). Something similar is also noted in Dostoyevsky's story 'The Gambler', a story which was itself something of a gamble for the author (he would have lost the rights to all of his work had he not delivered the story by the agreed deadline):

… it appeared to me that pure calculation means fairly little and has none of the importance many gamblers attach to it. They sit over bits of paper ruled into columns, note down the coups, count up, compute probabilities, do sums, finally put down their stakes and — lose exactly the same as we poor mortals playing without calculation. But on the other hand I drew one conclusion, which I think is correct: in a series of pure chances there really does exist, if not a system, at any rate a sort of sequence — which is of course very odd.[3]

It seems that to be a gambler one must be able to recognise and chase this sequence, as readily as a geneticist might a random mutation or a psychologist a casual word. But this chase can never result in a total capture, however. The goal is already subsumed within the attempt to attain it. The gambler is similar, in some ways, to Goethe's Faust: more interested in the possibilities of development than the attainment of riches. To return to 'The Gambler':

A gentleman … may stake five or ten louis d'or, rarely more; he may, however, stake as much as a thousand francs if he is very rich, but only for the sake of gambling itself, for nothing more than amusement, strictly in order to watch the process of winning or losing; he must not by any means be interested in the winnings themselves. When he wins he may, for example, laugh aloud, or pass a remark to one of those standing nearest to him, and he may play again, and then double his stake once more, but solely out of curiosity, to observe and calculate chances, not out of any plebeian desire to win.[4]

In such circumstances, the idea of winning or losing, victory or defeat, become meaningless, just as the idea of discovery had become within Borges' Library of Babel. Not to expect to win, or to discover, is not, therefore, something negative. Amongst so much craving, so much ambition, so much desperation, it is perhaps a useful thing to remember.

* * *

'The purpose of art is not separate from the purpose of technology.' — John Cage, 'Art and Technology', 1969.

* * *

You might, by now, be able to recognise some of the problems faced when trying to write about the work of an artist like Keith Tyson (although, it has to be said, that there are not many artists like Keith Tyson). It is impossible to write about the work, even engage with it as a spectator, without becoming part of its processes. Of course, one could just say that that piece is ugly and that this one is, well, less ugly, but this is to say very little indeed. Beckett once wrote admiringly of Joyce, and by implication himself, that his writing is not about something, it is the thing itself, and perhaps this is how we must approach the work of an artist such as Tyson. It happened just then, and you will have no doubt noticed it elsewhere, the appearance of other artists in this text, artists (and scientists also) whose methods share certain similarities with Tyson's. Again, this seems not only necessary, but unavoidable. Tyson's work always seems to lie somewhere else — we cannot just subject that sculpture or that painting to any meaningful form of formal analysis — and the presence of the Artmachine renders any form of biographical projection useless, assuming it ever has a use. His work operates as a matrix and is dispersed along itself; the best way of exploring it seems to be to create a parallel matrix of our own. We must feed into our

system the same influences, the same ideas, which Tyson has fed into his, or at least the ones which we imagine he has included. Of course, the results will be different, but once again this is a useful point: the procedure is a reiteration rather than a repetition and therefore the differences are as meaningful as the similarities.

There are a couple more elements which I think are needed to create a more productive matrix, a more productive language. We need more combinations within this work and so we must include those for whom the combination is their work, is the work, in order that we might absorb these connections also. This work is the creation of a language, a syntax, an assemblage according to certain rules, a combination of different elements, a composition of sorts. Perhaps it is unsurprising that we should turn to two authors…

The Marquis de Sade and Raymond Roussel are both infamous in their own ways. They are separated by over 130 years, in birth at least, although they are joined by the profound influence which they have both had on literature, particularly French, in this century (such is the promiscuity of influence). Indeed, it is their promiscuity which interests me here. In one sense, de Sade's is well-known, although I think that we would do well to reconsider its nature.

De Sade was obsessed with numbers, with calculations, with permutations. He saw the correspondences which he received from his wife during his various imprisonments as full of codes, *signals* he called them, which reveal the date of his release or the reinstatement of certain rights. His paranoid cryptomania even enabled him to find the genital measurements of his wife's imagined lover (imagined only by de Sade, that is) amongst the number of lines and characters within one of her letters. To read *120 Days of Sodom* is to enter a world of sexual obsession created by a perverted accountant. The end can only come about once all the participants have been accounted for, and the relevant arithmetic made, whether it is the 10 people massacred before the 1st of March, the 20 massacred after that date, or the 16 that survived and returned to Paris. If there are elements which trouble de Sade during these events, it is not due to their cruelty but to their being out of sequence. The fourth part of the book, which covers the 28 days of February, should contain the 150 murderous passions, yet at number 148 we read: 'The last passion.' 'But why the last?', de Sade writes to himself below, 'Where are the other two? They were all there in the original outline.' Elsewhere he notes to himself, 'Mistakes I have made', although once again these are structural rather than moral. Mathematics, and its numerical system, is a language and subject to a formal syntax like any other. One need only know a little about some of the sexual scenarios which de Sade devised to recognise the importance of procedure to him; it is hardly surprising that such a strict desire should also manifest itself in his use of language. If we talk of de Sade's promiscuity, perhaps we should not think of it as we would commonly, despite the fact that his promiscuity

manifests itself sexually. De Sade may devise some elaborate orgy — 'In all my days,' Juliette says, 'I have never seen a service so smartly done as that. The handsome members, once ready, were passed on from hand to hand, down to the children who were to insert them; they disappeared into the patient's ass hole; they emerged, they were replaced; and all done with an address, an alacrity impossible to describe' — but it is obvious that it is not sexual fulfillment, climax, that interests de Sade, but the smooth-running of the process, a form of perpetual motion (elsewhere he comments 'Nothing is so libidinous to see as the convulsive movements of this group made up of twenty-one persons'). De Sade's promiscuity is based upon combinations rather than a perceived immorality; a person may have several sexual partners simultaneously in order to increase the number of mathematical permutations, rather than any desire to transgress moral codes. Complex sexual relations become a form of algebra, taboos broken simpy a means of resolving certain equations. It is language which constructs these taboos and through the operation of language that de Sade breaks them.

While de Sade's relationship to Tyson is to a large extent abstract, that is, on the level of certain mental mechanisms only, the relationship between Roussel and Tyson also contains much which is actual, perceptible, to some extent real. Roussel was born in 1877, in Paris, as was de Sade; similarly, he was also to be a man of wealth. He published (or rather had published, at his own expense) a number of prose and verse novels, and also had produced a number

of his plays, but he was taken seriously by almost nobody during his lifetime except, perhaps, the Surrealists. It was only after his death (by his own hand) in 1933 that his reputation began to grow, in part due to the posthumous publication of *How I Wrote Certain of my Books* (1935), but also because of the acknowledgements made to his work by a generation of post-war authors such as Robbe-Grillet and Ionesco, and Foucault's critical book, *Death and the Labyrinth*, originally published in France in 1963.

Like de Sade, like Tyson, Roussel's work is also subject to the workings of certain procedures, certain methods. His most well-known was used in a number of his most important works — *Impressions d'Afrique, Locus Solus, L'Etoile au Front* and *La Poussière de Soleils* — and is described at the beginning of his explanatory text:

I chose two almost identical words … For example, *billard* [billiard table] and *pillard* [plunderer]. To these I added similar words capable of two different meanings, thus obtaining two almost identical phrases.

In the case of *billard* and *pillard* the two phrases I obtained were:

1. *Les lettres du blanc sur les bandes du vieux billard…* [The white letters on the cushions of the billiard table…]

2. *Les lettres du blanc sur les bandes du vieux pillard…* [The white man's letters on the hordes of the old plunderer…]

In the first, 'lettres' was taken in the sense of lettering, 'blanc' in the sense of a cube of chalk, and 'bandes' as in cushions.

In the second, 'lettres' was taken in the sense of missives, 'blanc' as in white man, and 'bandes' as in hordes.

The two phrases found, it was a case of writing a story which could begin with the first and end with the latter.[5]

While this structure may, to some extent, seem relatively straightforward, the results were anything but, hence Roussel's complete misunderstanding, and often ridicule, by Parisian society. Roussel's use of language goes far beyond this simultaneity, however. He would often take phrases and break them down into smaller combinations, creating new phrases through a purely aural syntax. For example, the folk song '*J'ai du bon tabac dans ma tabatière*' (I've got good tobacco in my tobacco pouch) can also become '*Jade, tube, onde, aubade en mat à basse tierce*' (Jade, tube, water, matt object, to third bass), elements which can be further reintegrated into a new situation, spread in combination with other elements, their origin lost.

The diaphanous image evoked an oriental landscape. Beneath the clear sky stretched a magnificent garden filled with seductive flowers. In the middle of a marble basin a jet of water in the outline of a gracious curve sprang from a jade tube.... Beneath the window near the marble basin stood a young man with curly hair.... He lifted the face of an inspired poet toward the couple and he sang a few elegies in his own fashion, using a megaphone of matt silver metal.[6]

'The process developed', as Roussel described it, as if by no direction from him; it appears as merely a syntactical inevitability.

It is not simply Roussel's methodology which bears such strong similarities to Tyson's, but the results of that methodology also. This is crucial, I believe, to any attempt to understand Tyson's project. Other important artistic machines, whether it be Borges' Library, or Cage's *I Ching*, seemed to produce work which was marked by a certain elegance, a certain restraint; although it may work along similar lines, the Artmachine's output is far more eccentric, we might even say vulgar, unrestrained by notions of aesthetics and 'good taste' (despite his dependence upon chance, Cage would often simply remove elements he didn't like).

This is where Roussel's precedence can play such an important role. One soon begins to read of objects, situations, which one can imagine as extravagant determinations of the Artmachine. There is the vast machine in *Locus Solus*, for example, a type of aerial pile-driver which creates a brightly patterned mosaic using only human teeth, each painlessly extracted element carefully chosen from amongst the polychromatic pile and placed appropriately, even taking into account, by some miraculous calculations, the strength and direction of every breath of wind. We might even be reminded of a specific work by Tyson, the photographer's tripod with the rejected stalks of a bunch of three cherries bringing to my mind, at least, *Bay City Pop-Colossus, Bulemic Still-life with Melons* (1996) in which a popcorn machine sits inside the waist of a pair of trousers, itself standing upon a snowboard attached to the top of a tripod, the three legs of which are rested upon bathroom scales. Pure coincidence of elements becomes irrelevant; what becomes important is the possibility of their assemblage. In turn, certain of Tyson's works could appear, at least, to be placed into one of Roussel's narratives. Consider *An emergency meeting of the doughnut assembly* which Tyson exhibited in Paris, appropriately, in 1996:

This bizarre piece looks more like an installation than a painting, but it has, however, been generated from the machine's painting algorithm. The specifications and positioning of the various grounds, framing devices, paint, additions etc. have caused this effect. The piece, as the title suggests, depicts an emergency meeting of the doughnut assembly, and has four main elements. 1) The dumping ballot (a painted box that protrudes from the wall on arms and releases paint into a series of channels. 2) The guest speaker (who sits on top of the dumping ballot craving applause). 3) The doughnut assembly (a series of cast forms that are roughly doughnut shaped and stand on a single thin leg). 4) The sugar fucker (an enamel painting on a bright white lightbox that leans against the wall attempting to distract the doughnuts). These elements installed in their various locations constitute the single Artmachine painting.[7]

We can find similar relationships in this exhibition also. *Experiments in Fusion 3 (Slow Breeding Stardust Reactor)* is the most explicit. Here we see a wall-mounted matrix, the elements made up of simple images, illustrations taken from magazines, as well as certain instructions or procedures. On plinths standing before the matrix are a number of strangely-formed objects. Their titles are given as a long list of numbers, functions and other elements, a description of the procedures of which they are the result. And so we have a combination of elephant, bicycle helmet, chimney, TV monitor, tribolite and 'something else'. If Tyson is interested in a form of mutation (and it is clear that he is), then here is an attempt to by-pass the restraints of Darwinism and species compatibility. Here, the breeding takes no notice of whether the elements are living, dead, or simply inert matter. What matters, instead, is the possibility of their combination within language, the promiscuity of their forms rather than their genes (and no gene could be this selfish). As in de Sade, taboos are broken in order to allow further combinations, more elaborate assemblages, rather than because of some immoral desire. And the objects themselves? What of them? As Roussel said, although it could just as well have been Tyson: 'Just as one can use rhymes to compose good or bad verse, so one can use this method to produce good or bad works.'

* * *

Some of the subjects dealt with are:
   Materialistic philosophy
   Archery
   Strategy
   Chariots
   Horses
   Elephants
   Elephant medicine
   Veterinary science
   War machines
   Trade
   Alliances
   Agriculture
   Zoology
   Cattle medicine
   Arboriculture
   Carpentry
   Athletics; development of the body

   Interior decoration
   Eloquence
   Drawing
   Writing
   Measurements
   Mineralogy; the science of metals
   Mathematics
   The science of precious stones
   Fortifications
   Tantrism
   Architecture
   Magic
   Anthropology
   Executions
   Chemistry
   Ichthyology
   Ornithology
   Herpetology
   Languages
   Treatise on the art of thieving
   Midwifery [8]

* * *

'One day down at Black Mountain College, David Tudor was eating his lunch. A student came over to his table and began asking him questions. David Tudor went on eating. The student kept on asking questions. Finally David Tudor looked at him and said, "If you don't know, why do you ask?"' [9]

The story is Cage's, but I'm sure he wouldn't mind (it's a story he shared with many people). Tudor was a pianist, for whom Cage often wrote, and a composer also. As an answer Tudor's is unexpected, the way that questions often are (one can only guess at the original questions although that seems unnecessary; Tudor's answer is the only question of relevance here). Its structure is simple, its rhythm implies certainty, like an adage, or a rule. It reveals its subterfuge only slowly, when its seeming familiarity begins to appear less so. (Wilde was the master of this form: 'One should not carry moderation to extremes.') Not to ask when one does not know implies that one must only ask from a position of knowledge; this was Cage's view of the exchange, certainly, and maybe he knew something here which I don't. However, it is not the student's lack of knowledge which Tudor is questioning, but rather his reasons for asking, it is his method of learning rather than what he has not yet learnt. Tudor's response concerns a process rather than a state of knowledge, which is why a question forms his answer. It implies a form of knowledge which cannot be arrived at through a simple question. This is what the story tells us, what its telling tells us: that many things cannot be told.

The approach must by now appear familiar; both impassioned and curious. It seems simple, and while there is a strong sense of research, it is not without contradiction (in appearance, at least). Tyson shares these things, of course, these workings are his own. Unlike the student, he is not searching for an easy answer; indeed, he seems not to be searching for an answer at all. It is the searching itself which fascinates Tyson. His work is not simply about dynamic processes, his work is a dynamic process, a regenerative process, a process which denies an answer, a proof (whatever next? Whatever could come next?) and is allowed to continue. His responsibility is that of any artist, according to Ananda Coomaraswamy, that is 'to imitate nature in her manner of operation', rather than copying appearances, to continue, and to continue to continue.

I am reminded of another of Cage's stories here. Xenia was Cage's first wife; by chance, it is also the name of Tyson's girlfriend, the artist Xenia Dieroff.

'Morris Graves introduced Xenia and me to a miniature island in Puget Sound at Deception Pass. To get there we travelled from Seattle about seventy-five miles north and west to Anacortes Island, then south to the Pass, where we parked. We walked along the rocky beach and then across a sandy stretch that was passable only at low tide to another island, continuing through some luxuriant woods up a hill where now and then we had views of the surrounding waters and distant islands, until finally we came to a small footbridge that led to our destination —

an island no larger than, say, a modest home. This island was carpeted with flowers and was so situated that all of Deception Pass was visible from it, just as though we were in the best seats in an intimate theatre. While we were lying there on that bed of flowers, some other people came across the footbridge. One of them said to another, "You come all this way and then when you get here there's nothing to see."' [10]

Jeremy Millar 1999

Not far to go now. I knew that it had to end this way, although I didn't know when it would be
Over, exactly. There were many different things that I wanted to mention here, many different
Subjects to raise. Perhaps the text is exhausting rather than exhaustive, its omissions no doubt
Yawning, and yet still the thought remains, nagging, troubling, the simple reiteration
That it didn't have to be like this, that it could have been different (although
How different we can only imagine). In another section of Borges' Library, down another route in
The forking path, we could have visited a multitude of different places, an
Infinity of possibilities. A different starting point, a different journey, although this, too, must
End. Perhaps in the end, coming to an end is not so difficult after all.
Knowing what to do next, that's the problem.

1. This text was commissioned by Galerie Georges-Philippe and Nathalie Vallois for Tyson's exhibition in 1997. Following the artist's interest in working within restrictive structures, I decided, arbitrarily, that the text would have ten sections and would consist of exactly 1000 words (the number I had been asked to write, albeit approximately). The knowledge that the text was to be translated into French gave me a perverse pleasure: would the translator attempt to keep to the designated number of words (indeed would this be possible?) or would they simply allow the discrepancy to remain testament to the problems of language?

I have quoted my own text here for a couple of reasons. Ask most critics, and they will tell you that they often find it difficult to write a text on an artist about whom they have already written. Now, I am not a critic although here I share their difficulties. Faced with the problem of repeating myself, I decided to repeat myself, and it was no longer a problem. Given much of what has been written in this new piece, the 'promiscuity' of an old text, consisting of ten sections, becoming one of the ten sections within this new text, had a certain appeal. Perhaps one day this whole text will become just one section of a much larger work.

2. *The I Ching or Book of Changes*, (Princeton University Press, Princeton, 1968), p.xxii

3. Fyodor Dostoyevsky, *The Gambler / Bobok / A Nasty Story*, (Penguin, London, 1966), p.38

4. ibid. pp.29–30

5. Raymond Roussel, *How I Wrote Certain of my Books*, (Exact Change, Boston, MA., 1995), pp.3–4

6. Michel Foucault, *Death and the Labyrinth — The World of Raymond Roussel*, (Athlone, London, 1987), p.42

7. Artist's description, distributed by Galerie Georges-Philippe and Nathalie Vallois, Paris, and Anthony Reynolds Gallery, London.

8. From 'The Acquisition of Knowledge' in Alain Daniélou (trans.) *The Complete Kama Sutra*, (Park Street Press, Rochester, Vermont, 1994) pp.46–47

9. John Cage, *Silence — Lectures and Writings*, (MIT Press, Cambridge, MA., 1967), p.266

10. ibid. p.46

WORKS
1994 - 1999

Artmachine Iteration:
"Bay City Pop-Colossus, Bulemic Still Life with Melons" 1996

Fibreglass resin, rubber, snowboard, tripod, bathroom scales, popcorn machine, popcorn.
Approximate overall dimensions 213 x 183 x 183 cm.

A. Jederman Collection N.A.

The identity of Keith Tyson's Artmachine is something of a mystery: for as a tool designed to erase an authorial voice, Tyson is keen to prevent transferring expectations of origin onto the machine itself. What he will reveal is that the Artmachine is a complex algorithm, a step-by-step computational rule, which has been specifically designed to generate proposals for an endless number of artworks. It treats the world as a giant database replete with an unlimited set of permutations as potential elements in any single piece. The Artmachine has the ability to tap every sphere of human thought in generating iconography for artworks: any idea or image which exists in the domain of knowledge, whether sourced from a library, a dictionary, an encylopaedia, or the internet, is within its reach. It makes decisions about every aspect of form and content : medium, scale, coloration, composition, title, metaphoric or narrative content, the time required to make the piece, iconography, gesture, even, if it is proposing a painting, the amount of pigment or matter to be applied to the ground. Tyson de-codes the Artmachine's coded specifications and then physically realises the given artwork, or "iteration". (Each piece is identified by an AMCHII prefix and a number).

In the early days - it came into being in1991 - the Artmachine was relatively crude and tended to propose a high proportion of unreasonable pieces - "Paint a photorealist picture of George Michael and the Queen waterskiing, paint it in deep water on a road" - thus condemning its emissary Tyson to a high level of failure. Over time, as Tyson has continually revised, honed, added and subtracted to its myriad layers of programming, the Artmachine has become more sophisticated. The 'rule' has developed to embrace more and more possibilities or 'variables', more and more systems of known logic (mirroring the way that art itself continually rewrites its own language and expands its own terrain).

The Artmachine is unpredictable in its proposals. It often generates wildly unorthodox collisions of imagery, materials and processes, seeming to eclipse the imaginative capabilities of a human author. And yet it is not a purely ludic machine. As Tyson says: "There is no such thing as pure chance, no pure randomisation in the phenomenological world -

there is always only unpredictability within given systems". The Artmachine, like throwing a die or spinning a roulette wheel or playing the lottery, can produce a breathtaking variety of possible results, and yet those results are never absolutely infinite or inexplicable or incalculable. The Artmachine metaphorises the fact that, deterministically speaking, everything that exists in the world can ultimately be understood in relation to apprehendable systems, or nexus of systems - whether, say, pure mathematics, or biology or probability theory or geology or evolution theory. And art, as a thing that exists in the world, just as a stone or a building or an atom or a telephone, is no less determined, even if its determinants tend to reduce to the psychological, the autobiographical or the experiential. The Artmachine is in one sense a peculiarly efficient artist, because its determinants are broader, because it has the capacity to draw on every extant idea and object in the world as the influencing factors of its art. Its sources are infinitely more expansive, and its artistic potential logically far greater, than that of an individual artist hampered by personality or temperament, and vulnerable to crises of inspiration or the punishments of negative criticism.

Like the work of its many Conceptual predecessors, the Artmachine prioritises idea over object, system over author. But what makes Tyson's invention so awesome is the epic scale of its potential, its ambition to do nothing less than embody the world's diversity and variability through the objects it produces. And this ambition is reflected in the Artmachine's Picassoesque prolificity - some 80 pieces realised each year, hundreds more waiting to be fabricated, or existing as allowable failures in the form of proposals; each work an intellectual and artistic challenge which may take up to 18 months for Tyson to interpret, devise, assemble and manufacture.

Structurally, it is impossible for the Artmachine to degenerate into repetition or formula or a signature style. For its repertoire is as varied as the history of art - from avant-garde performance to action painting, *art informel* to appropriation. Any exhibition of collected Artmachine works appears absurdly, wilfully, heterogenous, and this, although it makes no

sense to talk of essence, is perhaps the only essential characteristic of its art.

The Artmachine represents both pure purpose - its *raison d'etre* is to make art - and pure purposelessness - it is impossible to define the resulting works in terms of intention or meaning or teleology. Without recourse to notions of artistic agency, an Artmachine work is the ultimate, reified art object: pure product, pure material, pure matter - "it just depends on which way you put it together". There is no hierarchy within the *oeuvre*, no qualitative judgements to be made. The Artmachine overrides critical agony over the relative merits of gestural abstraction, slacker conceptualism, bad painting - for its works are simply more or less different to the last one. And it is pointless to analyse those differences in terms of the narratives of development and chronology which underpin Modernist thought. The Artmachine unhinges our conventional fixation on an individual artist's style, replacing a paradigm of individual development with one of endless diversification. Its works evade history: despite the Artmachine's own evolution over the last eight years, there can be no critical difference between an early and a late work. Its *oeuvre* does not get better or worse, more or less accomplished. There is simply, as Tyson adds extensions of logic to the labyrinthine Machine, an increased possibility for Artmachine works to differ from one another.

To state that the Artmachine undermines notions of significant form, is not to say that Keith Tyson's project is without significance. In replacing the idea of artistic progress with a model of pure diversification, the Artmachine is the precise mirror of a contemporary world irreducible to a single certainty or a single system of knowledge. It is a Borgesian, philosophical machine which charts those fine calibrations between control and chaos, logic and contradiction, purpose and chance, that give the world its peculiar dynamism. And further, although the Artmachine's conceptual identity is of more significance than any of the single objects it creates, it is impossible to overlook the fact that many of its works are inescapably compelling, whether in their absurdist poetry or their uncompromising aesthetics or their advancement of the artistic canon. Take the tiny thimble of paint dropped from 800 feet onto New

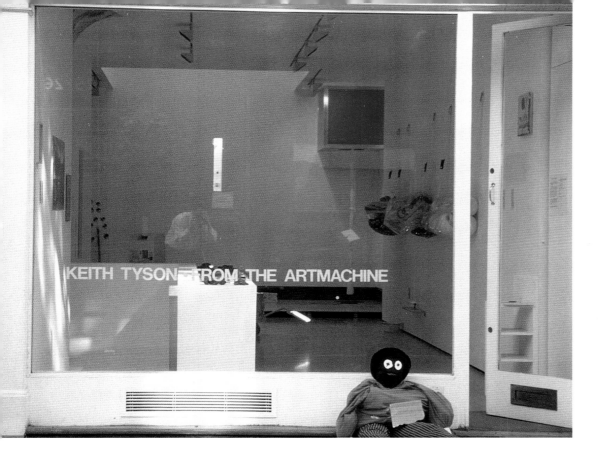

First gallery Artmachine exhibition
Anthony Reynolds Gallery, London 1995

York City in **New York Action Painting**, for example, and see how it reimagines *in extremis* the action painter's existential arena, here violently expanded from canvas to whole cityscape.

Or take **Molecular Compound No 1**, a piece comprised of 12 dispersed but related elements, which has the effect of radicalising traditional compositional relationships across time and space, as well as forcing the notion of the expanded field to a logical extreme. A single spherical nucleus hangs lonely in the gallery space, inscribed with information as to the identity and location of its companion elements - some are feet away, some miles away, some lightyears away. A salt 'n' vinegar flavour sculpture is floating down the Thames, current location unknown; a morse code message has been bounced by a laser torch to the moon; small paintings of Russian cosmonauts and English coalminers have been placed next to every piece of litter found in a nearby park; while an audio element - a recording taken at a street corner - is being dispersed over the airwaves by a local radio station. Or take the virtuoso handling of **Dual Workstations, 30 seconds late and early**, where each doubled element in two ostensibly identical assembled sculptures (replicas of someone's office workspace), are in fact separated by exactly a minute from the time they came into existence. Each photograph, for example, attached to the two pinboards, is taken exactly 60 seconds after the other - whether particles colliding in the Cern particular accelerator, or people waiting for a train at a London station. The newspapers were bought a minute apart, the regulation potplants result from two seeds planted precisely at a minute's delay - and so it continues, each item faithfully and slavishly realised to the Artmachine's instructions.

And what if, from within this conceptual system dedicated to pure diversification, and premised on aesthetic relativism, the ultimate paradox arose and the Artmachine were to actually produce work so utterly unimaginable and new, that it, in turn, catalysed a fresh epoch of artmaking? Logically that possibility, amidst all the other possibles and variants, must surely exist.

Kate Bush 1999

Artmachine Iteration:
"Mount, seal and encapsulate" 1998

Photograph, wood, plaster, paper, ink.
61 x 91 x 61 cm.

A. Jederman Collection N.A.

Expanded Artmachine Iteration:
"An expanded photographic encapsulation" 1998

Frosted perspex, telephone cable, 101 microprocessors, copper, LEDs, Sensatech electronic devices.
101 units (dimensions variable).

Private collection, Zurich.

A found photograph sealed in progressive layers of wood, plaster, paper, paint and a final layer of associations originating from the memory of the photograph inside the box.

Artmachine Iteration:
"Protective shield for use against the Atomic Spirits" 1997

Acrylic and oil on wood, NASA foil, survival bag, tinned food stuffs.
122 x 213 x 45 cm.

*Installation shot at The Approach, London, with works by Rebecca Warren,
Mike Kelley, Keith Tyson.*

Artmachine Iteration:
"Give us this day in the life" 1996-97

Mixed media on 366 wooden breadboards set into walldrawing.
Dimensions variable.

*Collection Pamela and Richard Kramlich, San Francisco.
Courtesy of Thea Westreich Art Advisory Services, New York.*

click to view

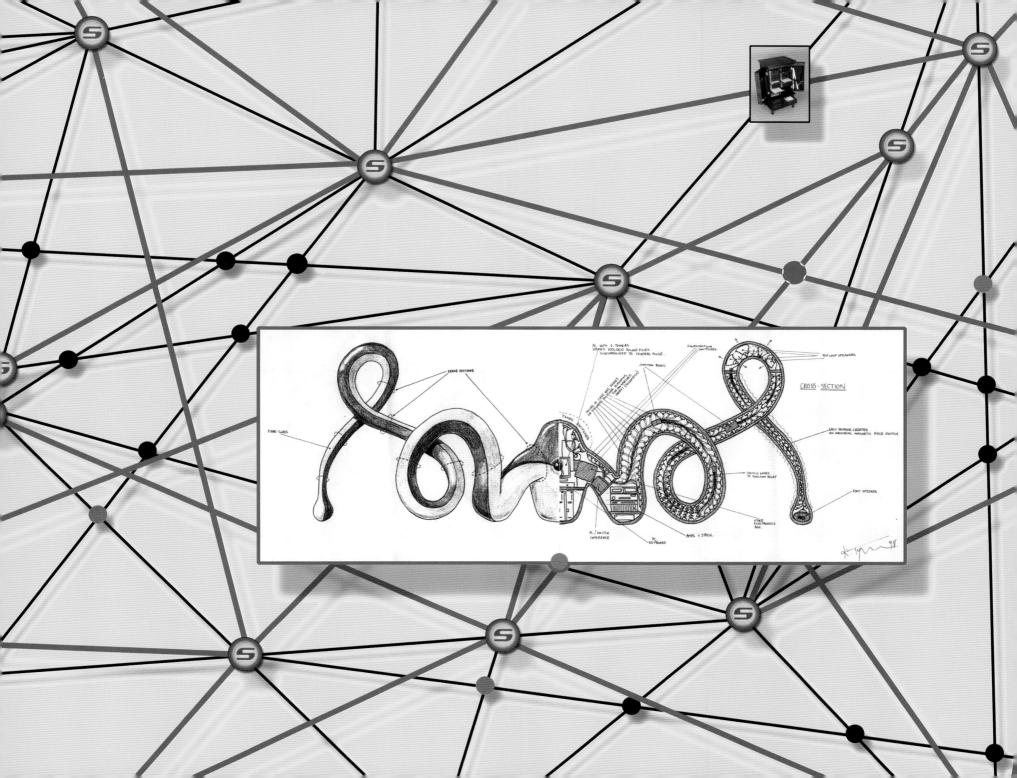

Recently I have been trying to create a form of drawing which instead of predicting some finished object, decribes a kind of dynamic of ideas, influences and generative forces that are struggling to become manifest in a piece. A conceptual model which evolves with an idea's development rather than simply illustrating a small stage of it. This fusion throws together different causal aspects; visual, mathematical, textual, historical, fictional, aesthetic etc.

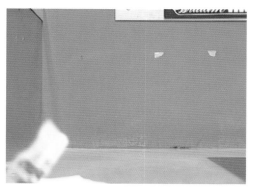

Artmachine proposal for Iteration
"Scubasculpture" 1995

A4 Laserprints taken from the edition
100 Artmachine Iterations 1996.

Iteration :	AMCHII• XXXVI
Title :	Scubasculpture
Format :	Sculpture
Status :	Proposed

Size / Duration :	approx. 500 x 500 x 500 cm.
Untitled number :	•
Series & Editions :	Unique
Hanging Specs. :	Floor
Location / Site :	Seabed for 16 years then any.
Documentation :	Map, certificate & proposal.
Date :	1995
Conditions :	16 year accumulation period.
Other variables :	An area rich in ocean life forms.

Brief description of proposed work / Reproduction of finished work

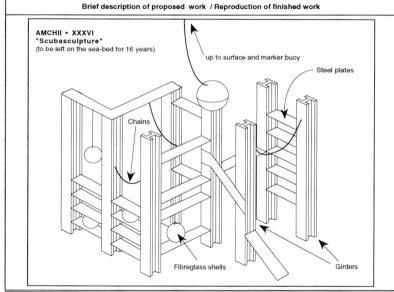

AMCHII • XXXVI
"Scubasculpture"
(to be left on the sea-bed for 16 years)

up to surface and marker buoy

Steel plates

Chains

Fibreglass shells

Girders

Notes :
Once commissioned and built, this steel and iron sculpture is submerged to the seabed (no specification as to which one) to weather and accumulate seaweed, limpets, mussels, barnacles and other oceanic matter for a period of16 years. After this period it is to be raised, dried, sealed and sprayed gloss white before being returned to its owner (that is the holder of the ownership certificate) for display as either an indoor or outdoor free standing sculpture.

PREVIOUS SPREAD

Artmachine Iteration:
"Angelmaker part 1; 15 seconds prior to the apocalypse, 100 views" 1996-98

Unique video.
25 minutes duration.

Artmachine repeater series:
"Purple parallel Ping Pong Pan Painting with Piracy Pendulum" 1997

Acrylic, silicone, plastic, emulsion on canvas, plastic pipe and cast plastic warships.
3 units, (each approximately overall dimensions 60 x 50 x 220 cms).

Dimitris Daskalopoulos Collection, Athens.

Artmachine Iteration:
"Grey Matter" 1996

Acrylic on M.D.F.
Dimensions variable.

Installation through 3 floors of
Laurent Delaye Gallery, London.

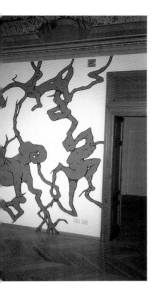

Artmachine Iteration:
"Grey Matter" 1997

Acrylic on M.D.F.
Dimensions variable.

Installation at Guarene Arte 97,
Fondazione Sandretto Re Rebaudengo Per l'Arte.

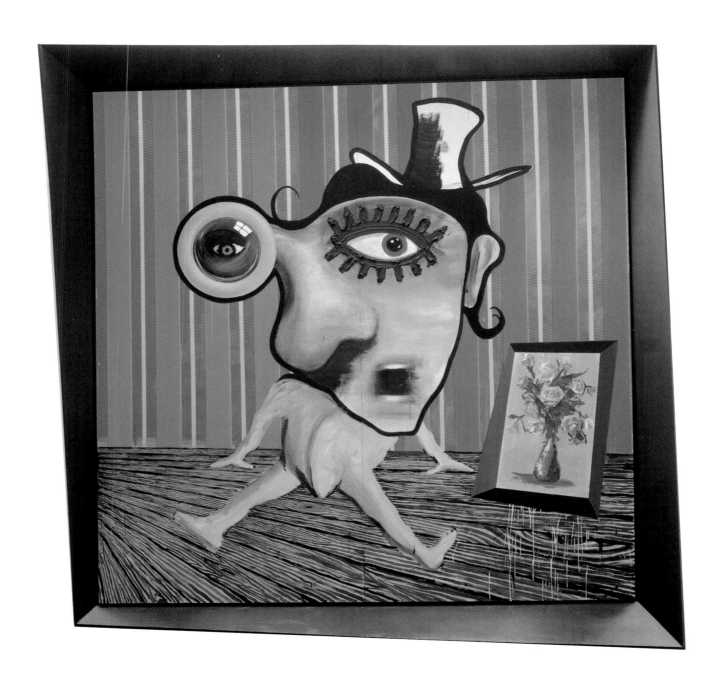

Artmachine Iteration:
"Untitled (chair)" 1997

Mixed media on underside of a broken chair.
50 x 35 x 47 cm.

Private collection, London.

Artmachine Iteration:
"The Prodigy" 1997

Acrylic on M.D.F.
Approximate overall dimensions 304 x 304 x 46 cm.

The Saatchi Collection, London.

Ostensibly two identical workstations with a bewildering array of images and objects that form a wide range recording of an individual's observable universe. On closer inspection, however, a difference becomes clear.

The compound state of each workstation is separated from its twin by an interval of exactly one minute (each item occurring 30 seconds earlier or later than a specified target date). In this way the workstations become a set of tolerances for a third implied workstation occurring somewhere between the two.

Artmachine Repeater Series:
"Dual Workstations (30 seconds late and early)" 1998-99

Wooden tables, cabinets, lights, maps, timers, photographic prints,
computer prints, drawings, mathematical models and diagrams,
newspapers, and various physical samples.
2 units (dimensions variable).

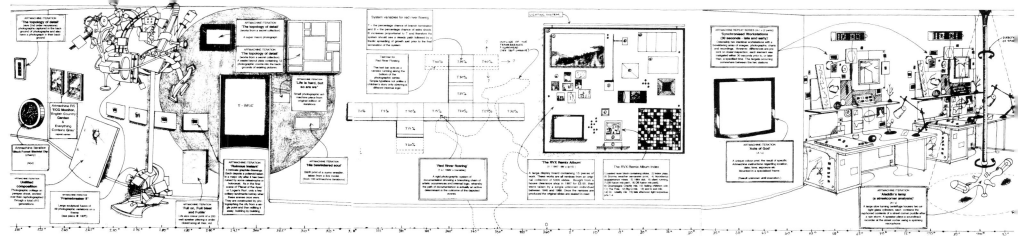

A Panoramic drawing showing the interior facets of a contradiction tolerant lens (studio version) 1998

Digicopy on draughting film, photographs and drawings.

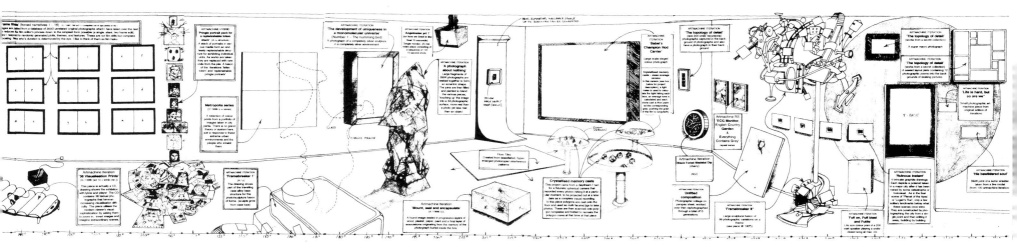

The drawing shows a 360° panoramic view of an installation of works in the virtual space of my imagination.
• I think of this whole exhibition as a large fragmented lens for photographing a complex reality, and each of the works in it, as constituting an individual facet of that structure (rather like a giant non-euclidian fly's eye). • I stood in the middle of the lens and turned around, drawing what I saw. • About 50% of the works are randomly generated by my artmachine system, the other 50% are new projects, works and systems that fill in some missing facets to the lens. • Eternally incomplete, the lens contains many infinitely recursive structures, yet a single facet may be little more than a texture or surface. • Using this contradiction tolerant lens, I am led through many different terrains, from the scientific and mathematical through to the mythological, emotional and abstract. • My travels through the lens are centred around photography and video in all their manifestations but the outcome of these pursuits are not necessarily photographic in form. • All the works depicted are currently in physical production.

A silver form is constructed within a completely silver environment. The only non-reflective points inside this silver egg are the small holes required for the lens and light source. The camera is set to autofocus and a large unique print is produced and sealed in a chrome frame.

ABOVE

Artmachine Iteration:
"The development of uniqueness in a monomolecular universe (number 2 - The Humming Bird)" 1998

Black and white photograph, chrome frame.
158 x 128 cm.

ABOVE RIGHT

Artmachine Iteration:
"A photograph about nothing (in and out of focus)" 1998

Mixed media 'touch up' over random photographic form.
244 x 152 x 152 cm.

A. Jederman Collection N.A.

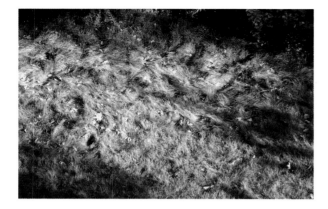

Artmachine Iteration:
"Shift" 1997

Field, leaves.
Dimensions variable.

PREVIOUS SPREAD

Artmachine Iteration:
"40 Stage repeater. AKA Double Crossroads Unit" 1997

Various event results stacked on welded steel base unit.
2 units, each 182 x 122 x 35 cm approximately.

Installation at Anthony Reynolds Gallery, London.

In the Repeater Series, I fabricate the iteration from a given instruction two or more times. The series has become an exploration of the limits of control within the artmachine process. Some repeaters have very exact instructions on every conceivable variable, while others require the instigation of a chaotic process at the time of fabrication. Depending on the type of commands generated the repeaters range from practically identical to unrecognisably different.

Iteration :	AMCHII• XCIV		Size / Duration :	approx. 2100 x 1300 x 500 cm.
Title :	Break		Untitled number :	•
			Series & Editions :	Unique
			Hanging Specs. :	Indoors
			Location / Site :	Any
Format :	Installation		Documentation :	•
			Date :	1995
			Conditions :	Dependent on pool-break
Status :	Proposed		Other variables :	•

Brief description of proposed work / Reproduction of finished work

This entire piece is based upon a single pool break.
A standard pool table is acquired and using 16 specially adapted pool balls –14 colours, 1 black ball and the cueball (see diagram below for ball modifications and markings), a break is made using the conventional 15 ball triangle set up. Each ball represents a separate Artmachine iteration, but its location within the space, its orientation, size and how it effects other pieces in its vicinity, are all decided by the break.
When the break has been made the positions are carefully recorded and marked, then the table top is sealed in a block of clear resin, to be lit by neon strips around the resin's edge.
A suitable site is now selected, scaled to the appropriate dimensions and the floor is covered in a carpet of green Astroturf. All the markings from the pool table are painted onto this carpet to provide the original layout at a greater scale.
The sealed pool table and the compiling devices are to be placed in the D.

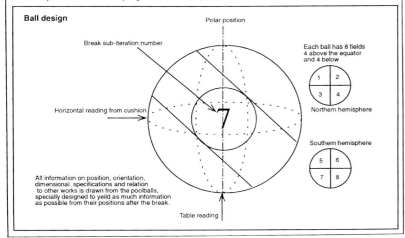

Ball design

Polar position

Break sub-iteration number

Each ball has 8 fields
4 above the equator
and 4 below

1	2
3	4

Northern hemisphere

Horizontal reading from cushion

7

5	6
7	8

Southern hemisphere

All information on position, orientation,
dimensional specifications and relation
to other works is drawn from the poolballs,
specially designed to yeild as much information
as possible from their positions after the break.

Table reading

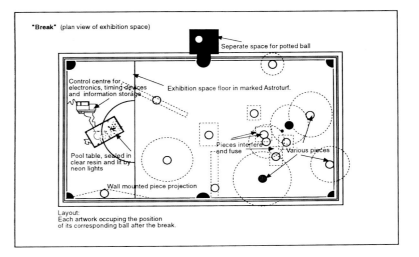

"Break" (plan view of exhibition space)

Seperate space for potted ball

Control centre for
electronics, timing devices
and information storage

Exhibition space floor in marked Astroturf.

Pieces interfere
and fuse

Various pieces

Pool table, sealed in
clear resin and lit by
neon lights

Wall mounted piece projection

Layout:
Each artwork occuping the position
of its corresponding ball after the break.

0	**Cueball**		8	**Black ball**
1	Lightbox display		9	Sculpture and paintings
2	Pit containing kinetic sculpture		10	Performance
3	Text piece (French)		11	Set of polaroid prints
4	Painting on Canvas		12	Video work
5	Painting on Board		13	Sculpture on table
6	Video work		14	Floor panels (large circle) with sculpture
7	Sculpture		15	Photograph

Notes:

The chart above shows the format of the respective iterations, however, with subject matter ranging from the political history of Taiwan to the development of new sculptural forms from fictional alien cathedrals, it is vir-tually impossible to predict what the pieces will actually look like until the break has been made and the information compiled. The only balls that are predefined are the cue and 8 balls, which will remain as fibre glass models of themselves at a larger scale (Unless, of course, they are touching other balls after the break, in which case they will fuse with the new iterations to form a hybrid work)

Artmachine proposal for Iteration "Break" 1996

A4 Laserprints taken from the edition 100 Artmachine Iterations 1996.

Artmachine Iteration:
"Angelmaker Part II, (the quadruped)" 1996

Electronically controlled multi-media installation.
792 x 610 x 381 cm.

Installation at the Institute of Contemporary Arts, London 1996.
Collection of Pamela and Richard Kramlich, San Francisco.
Courtesy of Thea Westreich Art Advisory Services, New York.

A telepathic request for collaborations was put out on February 1st 1995 which explained that all responses must be received in writing at the address given by the 1st of June 1995. All suggestions were to be painted on a 4' sq canvas. When the deadline arrived no such responses had been received.

Artmachine Iteration:
"Untitled (responses to a telepathic request for collaborations)" 1995

Nothing on canvas.
122 x 122 cm.

Private Collection, London.

Grids of randomly mutated images taken from Hungarian colouring books are used to form a cube containing a total of 54 paintings.

Artmachine Iteration:
"Super-Jumbo Colouring Book" 1997

Mixed media on canvas and wood.
155 x 124 x 124 cm.

Artmachine Iteration:
"An Emergency Meeting of the Doughnut Assembly" 1997

Perspex, rubber, steel, glass, flourescent lights, fibreglass resin, wooden 'dumping ballot', pour channels, funnels & 35 gallons of paint.

Installation at Galerie G-P. & N. Vallois, Paris.

Artmachine Iteration:
"Field" 1995

Cardboard box, model trees.
25 x 25 x 10 cm.

Private collection, London.

Artmachine Iteration:
"Rites of Spring" 1996

Mixed media.
61 x 20 x 25 cm.

Collection of Thea Westreich and Ethan Wagner, New York.

Artmachine Iteration:
"Untitled (flowerstall)" 1996

Colour print on canvas with engraved brass plate.
140 x 140 cm.

Private Collection Meyer Lausanne, Switzerland.

Artmachine Iteration:
"5 found frames for 5 found photographs" № 1 1998

Mixed media.
80 x 30 x 50 cm.

Private collection, Vienna.

Artmachine proposal for Iteration
"Timemachine (for travelling into the future at a rate of
9 192 631 770 periods of the radiation corresponding to the
transition between 2 hyperfine levels of the ground state of
a caesium - 133 atom per second)" 1995

A4 Laserprints taken from the edition 100 Artmachine Iterations 1996.

Iteration :	AMCHII• XV	Size / Duration :	150 x 250 cm diameter
Title :	Timemachine *(For travelling into the future at a rate of 9 192 631 770 periods of the radiation corresponding to the transition between 2 hyperfine levels of the ground state of a caesium–133 atom per second.)*	Untitled number :	•
		Series & Editions :	Unique
		Hanging Specs. :	Floor
		Location / Site :	Any
Format :	Sculpture	Documentation :	•
		Date :	1995
		Conditions :	•
Status :	Proposed	Other variables :	•

Brief description of proposed work / Reproduction of finished work

A) TIMEMACHINE
B) FIBREGLASS CASES • C) FIBRE GLASS HEAD UNIT • D) AERI-
AL • E) POWER UNIT • F) WOOD & FABRIC UNIT • G) WOOD &
ALI. UNIT • H) REST UNIT WITH DIGITAL DISPLAY • I) WOOD,
PLASTIC & ELECTRONIC CONTROL UNIT • J) BASE LIGHTS •
L) PIPE • M) MDF BASE.

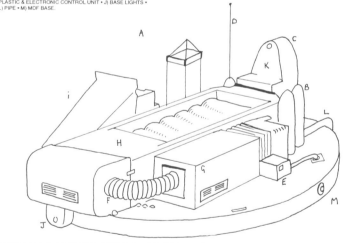

Notes :	This Machine actually travels at the specified rate into the future, but as all things travel at this rate*, its function is more meditative than transportive, isolating the temporal experience rather than accelerating it. A fusion of a sculpture and a time based piece (the long title is the scientific definition of a second after the original definition of: " 1 / 86 400 of the mean solar day" was considered too inaccurate to keep). *(With all the clauses of relativity aside.)

**The Rev. Remix Album 4
(ends and thumbs)** 1998

Unique prints, data storage disks
containing digital archive and the right of
reproduction for restoration purposes.
Dimensions irrelevant.

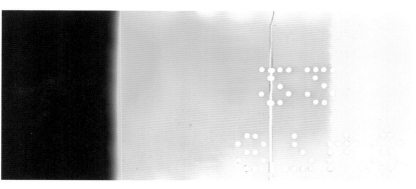

The Rev. Remix Project is an indexing project. All the albums in this series were constructed from an original collection of 5000 slides taken by a single unknown individual between 1945 and 1989. They were bought from a house clearance shop in 1997 for £5.00. They have been digitally scanned and sorted into various groups, many of the images appearing in multiple series and contexts. Once scanned the original slides were destroyed.

Tabletop Tales № 4:
"8 Dukes Mews, Centre of the Multiverse" 1998

ink on floorboards.
390 x 365 cm.

Tabletop Tales Nº 2:
"An Orbital Maelstrom For The Lost and Banished" 1998

Ink and graphite on found tabletop.
100 x 213 cm.

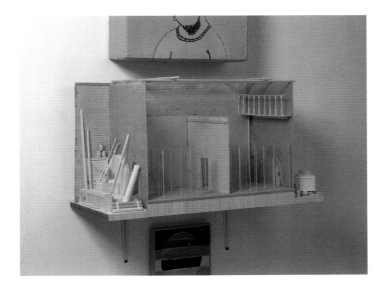

Bastardised Artmachine Iteration:
"Pringle Portrait Pack For A Replenishable Totem Stack" 1997

Potentially endless random portraits set in a vertical row from floor to ceiling.
Dimensions variable.

Details from series installed in Artist's studio, London.

Artmachine Iteration:
"The KFC Notebooks and the UCT" 1995

Every item on the Kentucky Fried Chicken menu cast in lead, computer animation
of a viral outbreak using the KFC outlets as its source, looped sound-track,
computer prints, photographs and case.
Dimensions variable.

Collection of Eileen and Michael Cohen, New York.

Artmachine repeater series:
"27 stage repeater AKA Double cellar painting" 1997

Mixed media on hardboard.
2 units, each 220 x 126 cm.

Private collection, Athens.

Artmachine Iteration:
"Rolling Stock" 1996

5 frames, shelf, set of photgraphs taken at specific intervals on a
train journey from Leeds to London.
18 x 183 x 13 cm.

Big Flower Press collection.

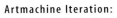

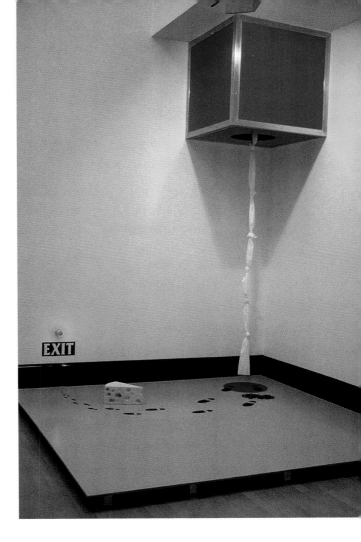

Artmachine Iteration:
"The Escapologist" 1995

Wood, steel, plaster, paint, lightbulb, knotted sheets.
244 x 244 cm x variable height.

Collection of Eileen and Michael Cohen, New York.

Forced Narrative 1:
"Witchtrials & Omens" 1997

Colour C-print.
90 x 120 cms.

Unique piece from a series of 16.

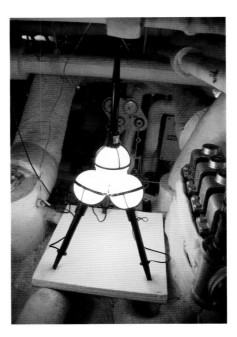

Expanded Artmachine Iteration:
Molecular Compound 1 1998

Ink on plaster, seven orbitals in various locations in the world.
25 cm nucleus diameter, 10,000 km maximum orbital range.

Installed at Delfina, London.

Expanded Artmachine Iteration:
Molecular Compound 2 1998

Ink, perspex, waterproof lights, thirty orbitals in various locations in the world.
100 cm quad-nucleus diameter, 10,000 km maximum orbital range.

Installation in the engine room of HMS. Plymouth, Birkenhead.

A monument to the present state of things

a public sculpture

In a Park, forecourt, or other public space stands a monument, not a modernist tower or ancient obelisk, but a simple arrangement of benches that form a meeting place on an area of raised ground.

In the centre of these seats the floor is cast in concrete, set into which are a series of internally lit vaults with flush glass lids that allow people to stand and view the contents.

At first glance, the items contained within each pit seem insignificant enough, a large pile of newspapers, some flasks of water, some transaction receipts, an electronic device, etc. Yet as the reverent lighting and text surrounding the vaults betray, these simple items form a junction that has consequences that spiral off exponentially; effecting the future in ways that we can only imagine.

This is not a monument to some past event or famous person that the world saw fit to commemorate, but to the state of things at the time of its viewing, however that future may appear or however far from the monument's construction it may occur. In fact, the older the monument becomes the more significant are its effects, to the point at which some viewers would not even exist without the monument's existence.

For like the now famous chaotic example of cause and effect, whereby a butterfly's flutterings have global meteorological consequences, each of these vaults represents the detritus of an activity that was executed solely to effect the future. The newspapers are in fact the result of purchasing every single newspaper on sale within 500 meters of a railway station 5 minutes before rush hour. The consequences of which are immeasurable as the commuters denied their papers are forced to look out of the window, perhaps decide not to watch TV tonight, to talk to the person opposite, etc. In short, to live a different life to the one they would have lived if they had acquired a newspaper. This difference is spread to all the destinations achievable by the trains and so on.

Each of the vaults holds similar residues taken from different aspects of the world. The water canisters contain a pint of water from each of the world's oceans, sealed to deny evaporation and causing an imperceptible drop in sea-level. Thus the monument effects financial, meteorological, geographical, political, technological, philosophical, municipal and cultural realities.

Of course, like any altar or significant artifact, there is nothing intrinsically special about the material items contained within the monument nor the events from which they are drawn. All events cause chain reactions, but while other events cause these effects by default, the monument's events occurred with the sole aim of indiscriminately effecting the future. Thus the monument becomes a node of focus, a reference point in time that encourages the viewer to ponder this interconnectedness of all things, the notions of chance and freewill and the inevitability of the monument's existence as it weaves itself into the destiny and fabric of the universe

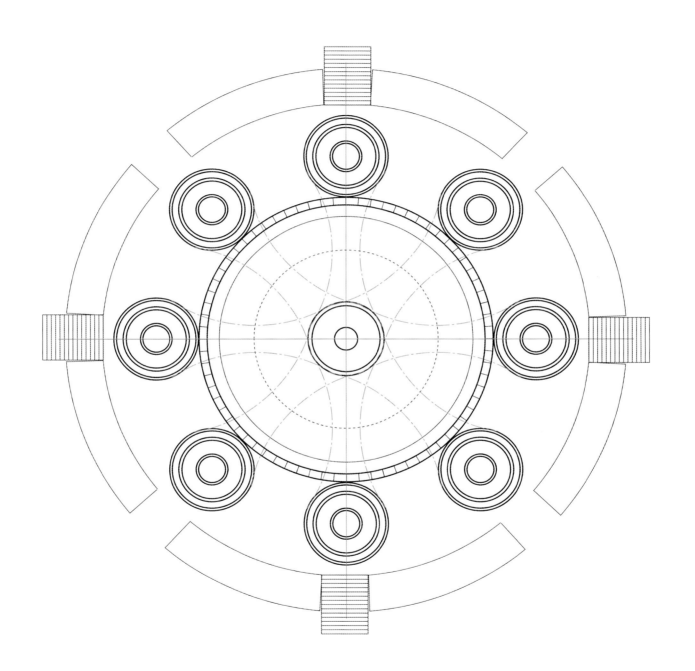

Map of the World part 5 (The Pleasure Park) 1994

Ink on paper, dart, video.
35 A2 sheets of drawing paper (210 x 416 cm).

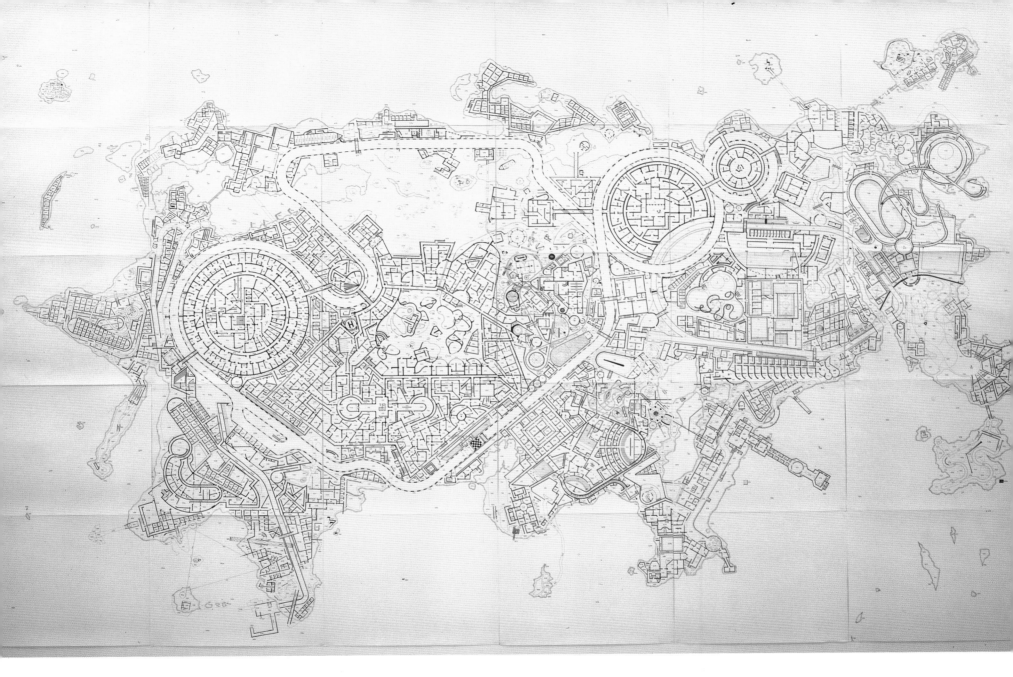

Artmachine Iteration:
"Inquiries into sequential cannibalism (super-twin airleap
with vibro-spider recorder) " 1996

Ramp, dress, architectural tension cables, paint glove, bouyancy aids, ink on wall.
Dimensions variable.

Installation at David Zwirner Gallery, New York.

In this piece, a ramp is placed 5 ft from the end of a long wall, at the other end the 'super-twin dress' is hung. Next the artist dons the vibro-spider recorder (a glove with nibs on the fingertips that pumps paint as the artist runs). Starting at the super-twin end the artist places the vibro-spider against the wall and runs at full speed towards the Airamp, leaving five coloured traces in his wake. The resulting installation resembles a hybrid of a giant seismograph, a minimal wall drawing and a 1970s motor-cycle stunt jump.

On a windy morning in 1998 a set of balloons carrying a small payload of acrylic paint was launched from a New York street. When the balloons reached approximately 800 ft the paint was released over the city. Thus the whole city became the canvas for a very large but untraceable 'Action Painting'. The rest of the day was spent in a futile attempt to find and match paint traces on the sidewalks and buildings. Although the owner of this piece receives a unique set of documentary photographs, the actual work remains this large unviewable painting, in whatever state it may presently be, over the streets of Manhattan.

Artmachine Iteration:
"New York Action Painting (detail)" 1998

Acrylic on Manhattan.
Dimensions unknown.

Collection Blake Byrne, Los Angeles.

full of laundry

The exhausted breathing of two reindeer stags th
are starving to death due to their antlers becomin
locked together during the rut.

**A capital city compressed to the
size of a marble and swallowed.**

The number 5875420091643245008646

d love po
e in autumn

Three elderly ladies watching a television
gameshow while drinking tea, each one
thinking of something else.

A teenage sunbather.

The complete area covered by the sum of the
internal space inside every letter 'O' that has
ever been written or printed.

dow cast by the central
f the Circus Maximus on
summer evening sometime
nd century A.D.

$\int \sqrt{2^n} \left(2.7i - 6 \right)$

Snow on the top of a bus shelter as
seen from the window of a London
double-decker bus.

A mental image of the burning bush
created by the mind of a nine year old
girl in an English church in 1796.

The sound of cattle at the saltlick

hird pillar from the right when facing

The path surrounding

Claudio Monteverdi's pancreas.

9495819875461 2645

A red and green tent pitched underneath an
electricity pylon on the outskirts of Leicester.

A dr
figh
pas
hop

The smell of dusty ground
soaking up the rain.

**A bullet perpetually ricocheting off
the interior walls of a giant empty
iron vessel.**

The sights seen by an archaeopteryx
during a 30 second flight on a hot day
in 176,023.809 B.C.

The space between the roof of Vasco da Gan
mouth and his tongue when pronouncing the
'T'.

A cloud of cream forming in a cup of coffee

A 4 cm scratch on the surface of a solid
block of frozen milk measuring 125 Km long
x 125 Km wide x 125 Km high.

A switch that utilizes the enantiomers of
limonene to make random reciprocations
and has thus acquired the slang name of
'the orange and lemon flipper'.

1010100010101011011

KEITH TYSON

1969
Born in Ulverston, Cumbria

1984-89
M.E.C.S (Mechanical, Engineering Craft Studies)
Barrow-in-Furness College of Engineering.

1989-90
Carlisle College of Art

1990-93
University of Brighton; Alternative Practice

1996
ICA Arts and Innovation Award 1996

Individual Exhibitions

1995
From the Artmachine, Anthony Reynolds Gallery, London

1996
David Zwirner Gallery, New York

1997
Anthony Reynolds Gallery, London
Galerie Georges Philippe and Natalie Vallois, Paris

1999
Delfina, London

Group Exhibitions

1990
Passive Voyeurs, Stanwicks Theatre Complex, Carlisle

1993
The Space Between, Gallery Fortlaan 17, Gent
The Observatory, Anthony Reynolds Gallery, London
Spit in the Ocean, Anthony Reynolds Gallery, London

1994
Untitled Streamer Eddy Monkey FullStop Etcetera, Anthony Reynolds Gallery, London
Streamer *Mute*, Pilot Edition, p IV, V, Winter

1995
Institute of Cultural Anxiety, Institute of Contemporary Art, London
Disneyland After Dark, Uppsala Konstmuseum, Uppsala (catalogue)
Night and Day, Anthony Reynolds Gallery, London

1996
Pandemonium, Institute of Contemporary Art, London
Surfing Systems, Kasseler Kunstiverein, Kassel and tour (catalogue)
White Hysteria, Contemporary Art Centre of South Australia,
Disneyland After Dark, Kunstamt Kreuzberg/ Bethanien, Berlin
In Passing, The Tannery, London
Madame ma conscience, Galerie Georges-Philippe and Natalie Vallois, Paris

Replicators, http://adaweb.com

1996
On a Clear Day, Cambridge Darkroom, (First Site, Focal Point, John Hansard Gallery, ICA, Middlesborough Art Gallery) (catalogue)
Monsieur ma conscience, Friche Belle de Mai, Marseilles
Superstore Deluxe, UP & Co., New York

1996
Art and Innovation Shortlist Exhibition, Institute of Contemporary Arts, London

1997
Dissolution, Laurent Delaye, London
Low Maintenace & High Precision, (Hales and) 127 Deptford High Street, Lewisham, London.
Guarene97 Fondazione Sandretto Re Rebaudengo per l'Arte, Turin (catalogue.)
Private Face-Urban Space, Gasworks, Athens; L. Kanakokis, Municipal Gallery of Rethymnon, Crete (catalogue.)
Sarah Staton's Truly Supastore, Cornerhouse, Manchester

1998
What's in a Name?, Anthony Reynolds Gallery, London
Bad Faith, 3 months gallery, Liverpool
Show me the money, 8 Dukes Mews, London
U.K Maximum Diversity, Benger Areal, Bregenz, Galaerie Ursula Krinzinger, Vienna
Diving for Pearls, H.M.S. Onyx, Birkenhead
Klink Klank, H.M.S. Plymouth, Birkenhead
It's a curse, it's a burden, The Approach, London
Holding Court, Entwistle Gallery, London

Writings

1993-

"Streamer", continuous text and illustration sequence running through exhibitions, magazines, internet, etc.

1995

"Around the Compendium in 54 Aphorisms, (Including Jokers)", in *Mute*, No 1, p. IV, V, Spring

Bibliography

1994

Adrian Searle, *Time Out*, 7 September

1995

William Feaver, 'A strange ghetto of allusions', *The Observer Review*, 8 January

Richard Dorment, 'Science Friction', *The Daily Telegraph*, 11 January

Simon Grant, 'Institute of Cultural Anxiety', *Art Monthly*, February

Stuart Morgan, 'the future's not what it used to be', *Frieze* March/April, No.21

Adrian Searle, 'Keith Tyson', *Time Out*, July 12-19, p.46 *The Times*, Monday 10 July

David Beech, 'Strange Company The Brady Bunch Movie and Keith Tyson, *Artifice*, Issue 3

1996

'Oxygen of publicity', Londoner's diary, *Evening Standard*, Thursday 7 March

Jonathan Romney, 'The in crowd', *The Guardian*, Wednesday 13 March

Sarah Kent, 'Video Games', *Time Out*, 12 March

Rosanna Negrotti, 'Pandemonium', *What's On*, 27 March

Sean Dower 'Video Review (Keith Tyson) *Zap Video Magazine* Spring issue

Sacha Craddock, 'Around the galleries', *The Times*

Olaf Furniss, 'Weird Art', *I-D*, April

Emily Tsingou, 'Night and Day', *Zingmagazine*, Spring

Louisa Buck, 'Silver Scene', *Artforum*, p.34-36

Nick Haughton, *Mute*, no.5

Jerry Saltz, *Time Out* New York, 15 July

Grace Glueck, 'Keith Tyson', *The New York Times*, 19 July

Glenn Brown, 'The Artmachine', interview with Keith Tyson, *Bomb Magazine*, Autumn (ill.)

Jim McClellan, 'The Art of the Implausible', *The Guardian*, Thursday 31 October (ill)

Peter Schauer, 'Britpack's Brilliant Bargains', *Art Review*, Autumn, p.26-27 (ill.)

Artists Newsletter, December, p42 (ill)

1997

ID Magazine, Talent Issue, January.

David Barrett, 'Dissolution', *Art Monthly*, April (ill.)

Martin Herbert, 'Keith Tyson', *Time Out*, 21-28 May (ill.)

Dave Beech, 'Keith Tyson', *Art Monthly*. June, p.38-39, (ill.)

David Burrows, 'Low Maintenance & High Precision', *Art Monthly*, September, p.39, 40

Kate Bush, 'Keith Tyson', published in 'Guarene Arte 97' catalogue, Ed. Fondazione Sandretto Re Rebaudengo per l'Arte.

1998

Dave Beech, 'Another Tyson Ear Bending', *everything* 2:3, p.18-21, 31 (ill.)

1999

Louisa Buck, 'Our choice of London contemporary galleries', *The Art Newspaper*, No.88, January, p. 70

David Musgrove, 'It's a curse, it's a burden', *Art Monthly*, February, p. 37

I would like to offer a special thank you to all those who have supported the making of this catalogue and the exhibitions, works and concepts contained within it (in no particular order): Xenia K. Dieroff, Mrs. F. E. Birkett, Mrs. A. Rigby, Anthony Reynolds, David Gilmour and Delfina, Alan Ward, Jeremy Millar, Kate Bush, Georges-Philippe and Natalie Vallois, David Zwirner Gallery, Chris Newman and Sensatech, Benedicte Delaye and Tristram Pye, Nick 'it is what it is' Dowdeswell, Pete White of FXP, Thea Westreich Art Advisory, London Electronic Arts, Wilson & Woods, Simon & Pauline @ Mute Magazine, Glenn Brown, Gavin Wade, The Henry Moore Foundation, Tim Olden & The Worldwide Supermarket of Sound, Dave Beech, Ethan Wagner, Colin from Redifusion Simulation Brighton, Jake Miller, Goshka & Matt, Laurent Delaye, The Institute of Contemporary Arts, and anyone else who has taught me, bought me or sought me, and finally Mr. Newnam of (the no longer existing) Broughton Road School, Dalton - in - Furness, who taught me how to draw a radiator stoptap in 1976 and began the flow of works that has continued ever since.   Keith Tyson.

This publication has been supported by
The Henry Moore Foundation